Song of the Cicada

of the

by Cal Martinez
illustrated by Mary Teichman

Harcourt
SCHOOL PUBLISHERS

Printed in China

ISBN 10: 0-15-350499-4
ISBN 13: 978-0-15-350499-0

Ordering Options
ISBN 10: 0-15-350333-5 (Grade 3 Below-Level Collection)
ISBN 13: 978-0-15-350333-7 (Grade 3 Below-Level Collection)
ISBN 10: 0-15-357486-0 (package of 5)
ISBN 13: 978-0-15-357486-3 (package of 5)

2 3 4 5 6 7 8 9 10 985 12 11 10 09 08 07

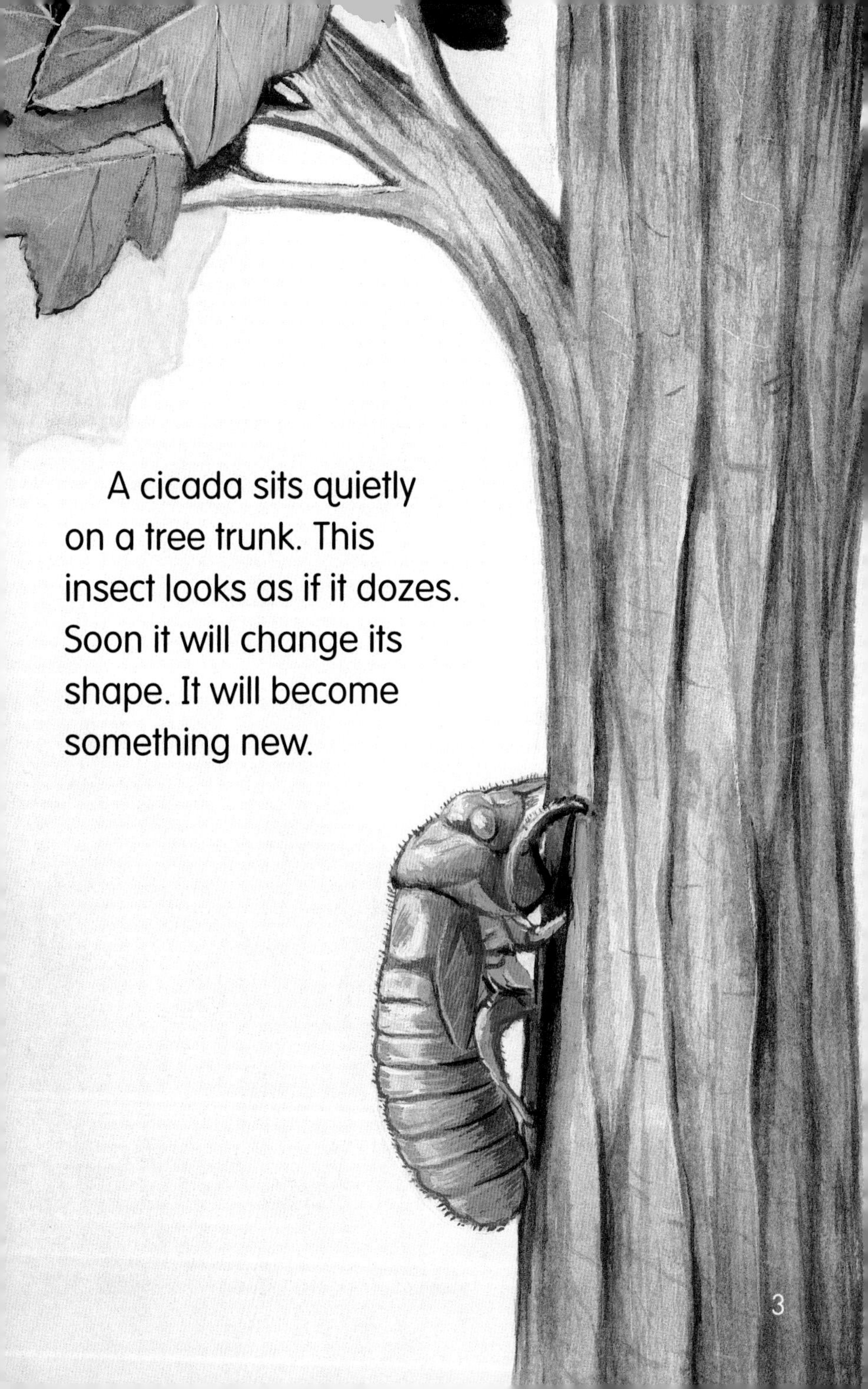

A cicada sits quietly on a tree trunk. This insect looks as if it dozes. Soon it will change its shape. It will become something new.

This cicada has already lived seventeen years, but it is not yet fully grown. It is still a nymph. That means it is still a baby. It is getting ready to grow one last time.

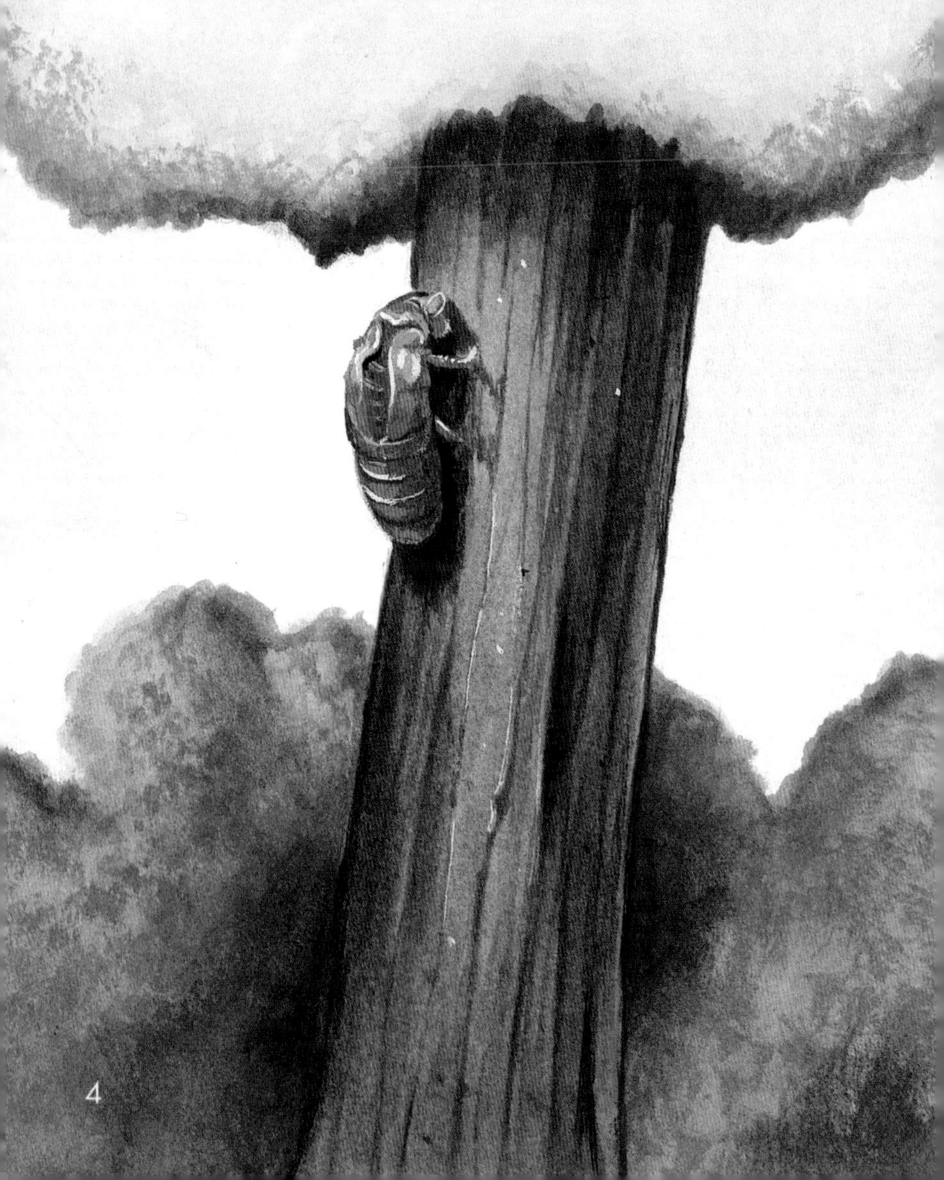

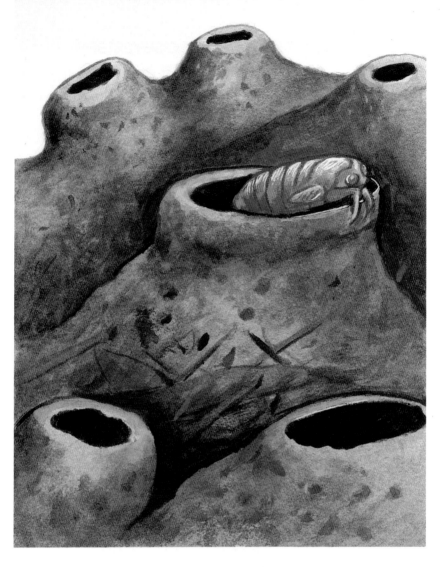

Very early this morning, the cicada
nymph dug a tunnel from under the ground.
It crawled from a small hole. It had been in
the ground for years.

The nymph fell from a tree seventeen summers ago. Its mother had laid eggs in a small hole in the tree branch. About two months later, the eggs hatched. The tiny nymph crawled out. Then it fell to the ground.

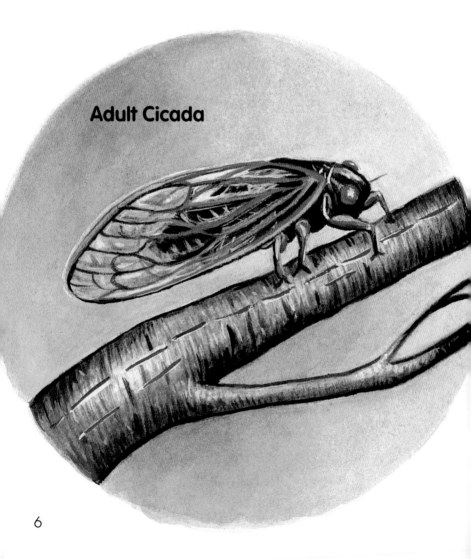

Adult Cicada

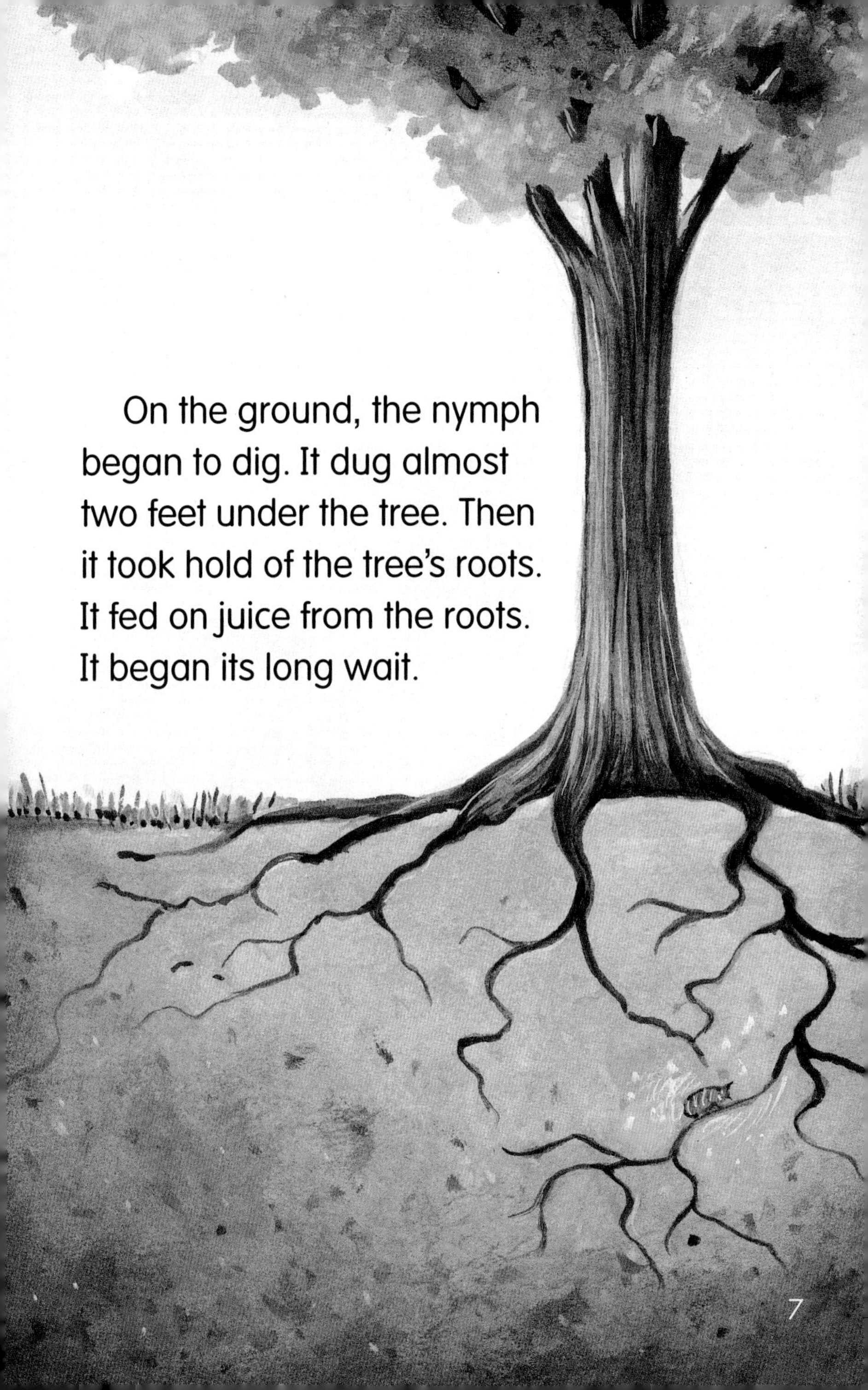

On the ground, the nymph began to dig. It dug almost two feet under the tree. Then it took hold of the tree's roots. It fed on juice from the roots. It began its long wait.

Annual cicadas appear every year. Some cicadas appear every thirteen years. The seventeen-year cicada comes every seventeen years. It lives longer than any insect in North America!

Annual Cicada

Seventeen-year Cicada

The cicada nymph grew as years passed. It outgrew its skin, and it formed a new one. Still the nymph waited. One warm day, it was time to come out! No one is sure how cicadas know when the long wait is over.

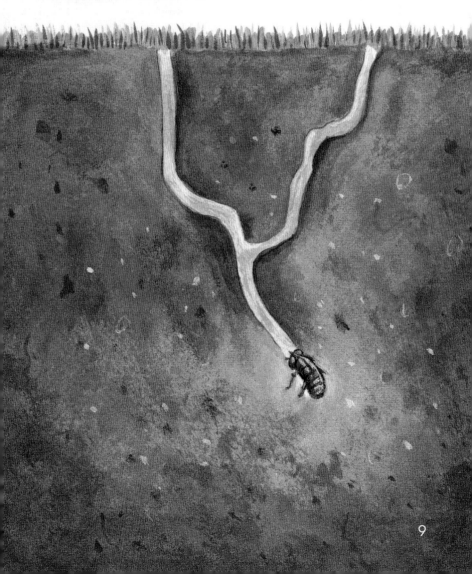

The cicada nymph let go of the roots. It dug a tunnel up to the surface. Sometimes cicadas push up small mounds of dirt around their holes. Then they slowly climb up trees or tall weeds.

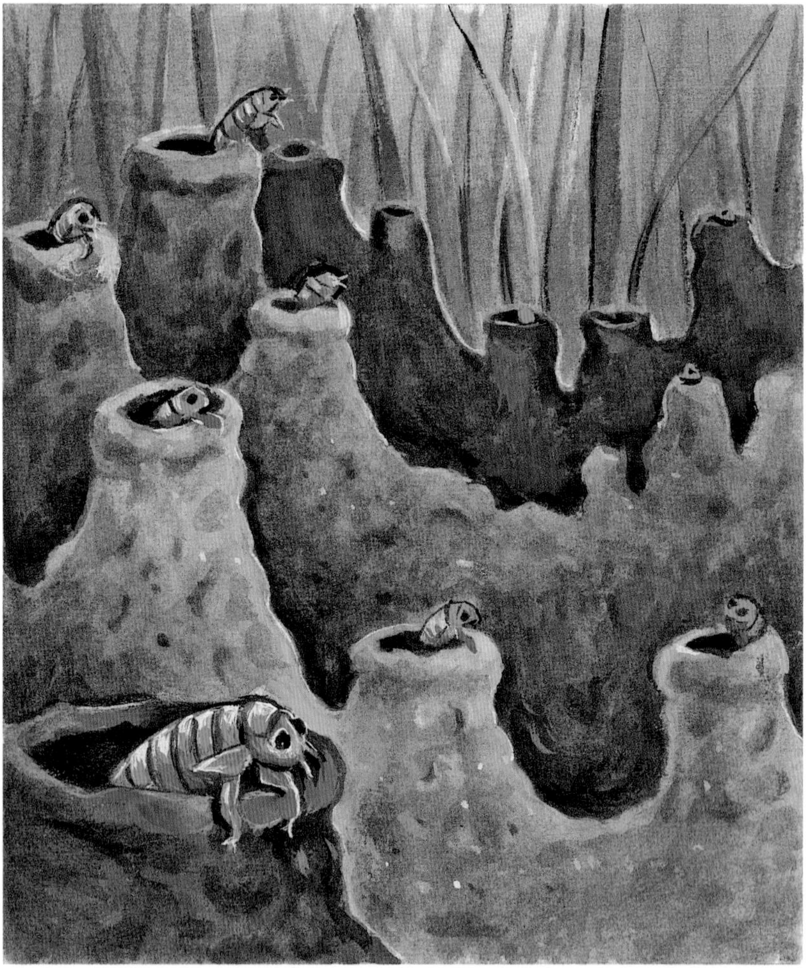

The cicada changes one last time. With great effort, it sheds its skin. It leaves its old skin on the tree or weed. You can see every detail of the nymph's shape in the old skin. Millions of cicadas have done the same thing.

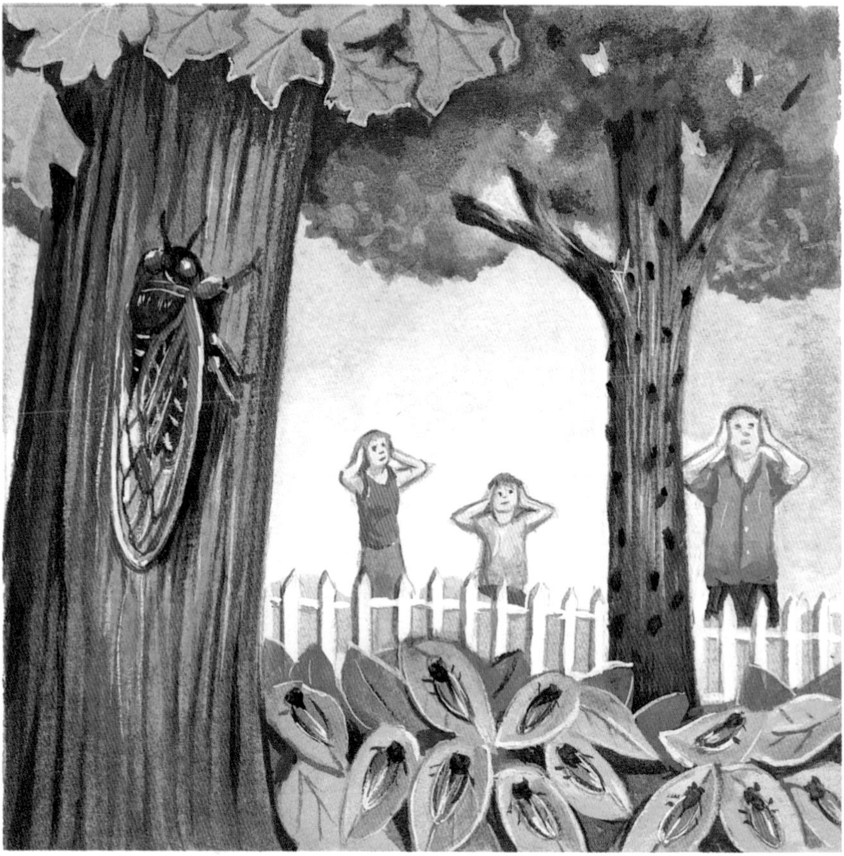

Now the cicada looks different. It is an adult with wings. It waits for its new body to dry. Then the males begin to sing. They call the females. The sound from millions of cicadas is everywhere, and it is loud. Cicadas are not nocturnal, but the loud buzz goes on late into the evening.

Males and females fly in swoops and circles to find each other. Over the next days, the song and the fluttering flights go on and on. There may be thousands of cicadas in one small backyard. Many birds and animals eat the cicadas. There are so many cicadas, though, that millions are still left.

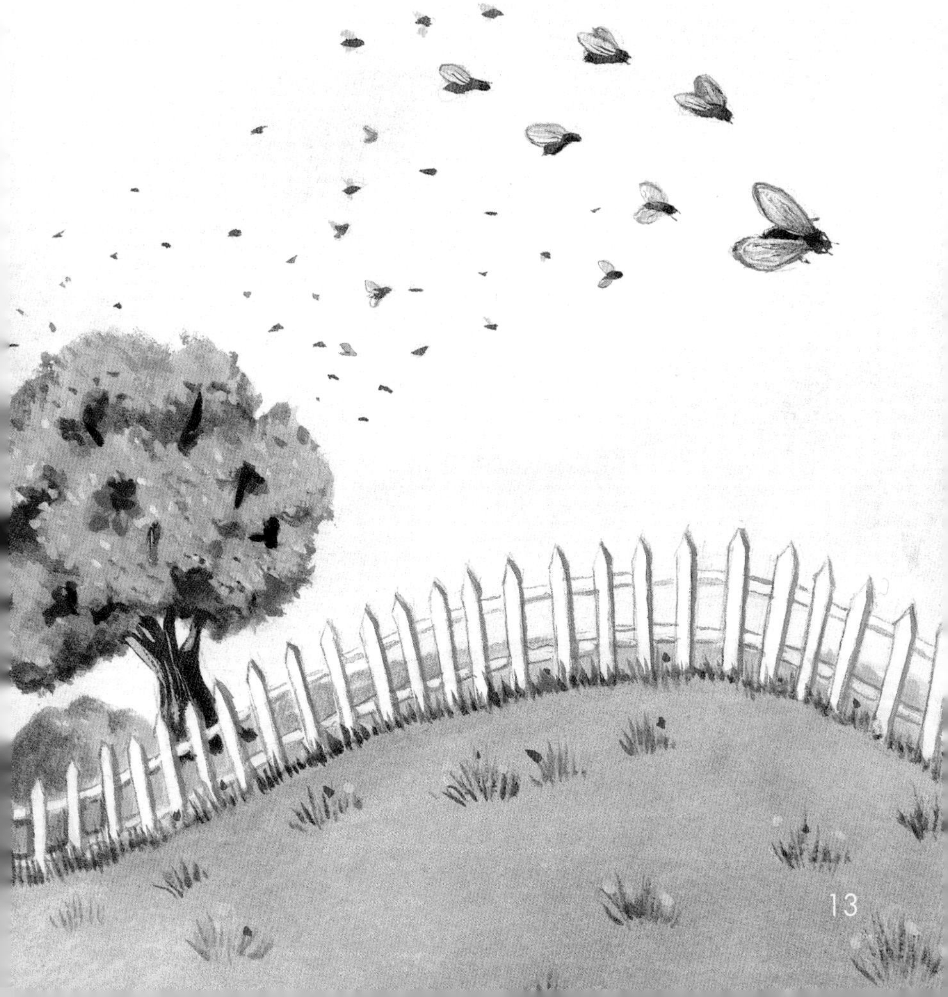

The cicada's life is nearly over. After mating, females cut holes in branches to lay their eggs. The males and females live a short while and then die. Their eggs will hatch. New nymphs will go into the earth again. They will wait another seventeen years. Then the amazing song will return.

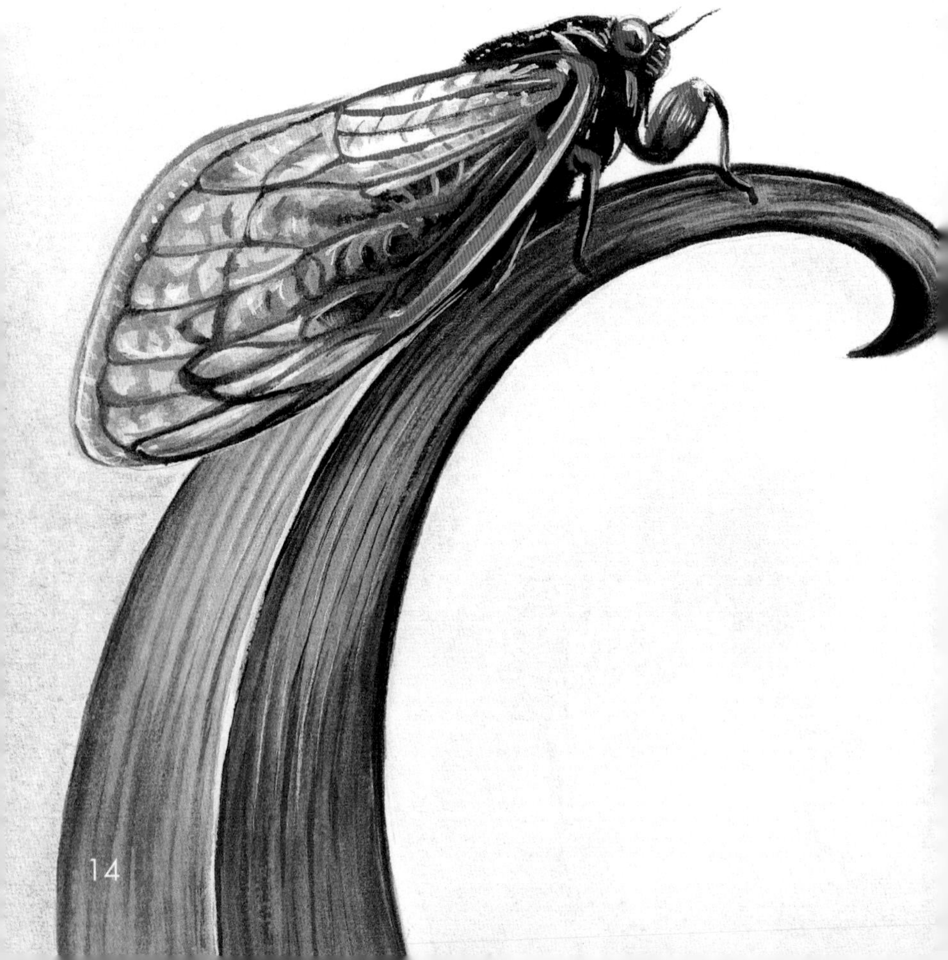

Think Critically

1. Look at the pictures in this book. What are some differences between cicada nymphs and cicada adults?

2. What do humans not know about the cicada's life?

3. How might birds and animals be helped in years that cicadas arrive?

4. What might happen if the tree the cicada nymphs were waiting under died?

5. Why do you think the author might have written this book?

Science

Make a Drawing Draw a picture of a tree. Using what you have learned in this book, show the life cycle of a seventeen-year cicada. Use arrows to show where the cicada lives at each stage of its life.

 School-Home Connection Seventeen years is a long time. Talk to friends and family members who can remember seventeen years ago. What are some of the things that have changed since then?

Word Count: 480 (487)